PADSTOW
THROUGH TIME
Malcolm McCarthy

AMBERLEY PUBLISHING

North Quay, _c._ 1909
Pictured _c._ 1909, the _Rhoda Mary_
is lying alongside the North Quay
undergoing a refit or repairs.
Shipwrights are on planks laid
along her port side, having stripped
her gunwales down. At this time,
the schooner was owned by
the Allport family and she was
working out of Padstow. The days
of shipwrights working on wooden
ships are, sadly, gone, and Peter
'Dasher' Reveley was the last one
working on wooden vessels in the
port. Coincidentally, 'Dasher's' great
grandfather, John James Reveley, is
on his boat, PW8 _Bessie Ellen_, which
can be seen in the foreground.

First published 2009

Amberley Publishing Plc
Cirencester Road, Chalford,
Stroud, Gloucestershire, GL6 8PE

www.amberley-books.com

ISBN 978 1 84868 296 2

British Library Cataloguing in Publication Data.
A catalogue record for this book is available from
the British Library.

Typeset in 9.5pt on 12pt Celeste.
Typesetting by Amberley Publishing.
Printed in the UK.

Introduction

Whilst having a quiet pint at the Social Club, young Thomas Murt approached me and said, 'Hey Malc, you knaw what would be good? A book a photas showing Padsta how it was and how it is now, you knaw what I mean? It would be really interestin.' I poo-pooed the idea at the time, but on mulling it over I decided that if the youngsters were interested then why not? And that was the birth of this little book.

I must apologise straight away, as I have to reuse many photos that have already appeared in my old photograph books, and this may prove a little irksome to some. I am afraid, however, that this was inevitable, as I am finding it so hard to find any new images. If anyone out there has any old photographs then please let me know. On this note I would like to add a special thanks to Lambert Dive and Michael Champion who have both recently sent me photos. I have also been asked to produce one of these little books on St Merryn, so I am on the lookout for any St Merryn parish images.

On walking the streets of Padstow lately, armed with my camera and folder of photos, my wife Pat dutifully following on with Harry our dog, Pat being in charge of the folders has been an invaluable help. On wandering around, I began to realise that a lot of the major changes have happened in my lifetime and were, luckily, photographed either by myself or my late father. As often happens in these cases, you realise the loss of something when it's too late, hence a lot of the photos are during or after demolition of buildings and not before — with hindsight, before might have more useful! Fortunately, George Barnes was also taking photos in and around the '70s and '80s. He passed on some of his negatives to me a few years ago and has kindly given permission for these to be used.

I have not concentrated on the new Harbour Gate, the shuttering of the Inner Quay walls, the lifeboats, the Kernow Players or the fire brigade, as any of these could warrant books of their own. This book is aimed at recording some of the changes to the town in order that that local people can appreciate what is happening to their town, gradually but quite dramatically. Some changes are not covered as I have no relevant photograph of the Drill Hall, the Public Rooms or the British Legion Hut, to mention but three. We, as local residents, have to be more vigilant to subtle changes in Padstow, such as is happening at Cove at the moment. A gate has been placed across the public footpath, giving the impression to the uneducated walker that there is no right of way. We must stand united and resist such changes, protecting our rights over the ancient footpaths.

Change can be a good thing; I will leave it to the readers to decide for themselves if this is the case.

For the visitor, the order of the pictures is as if walking from Dennis Hill along Dennis Road up to the Old School; then through the Lawns, along Hill Street, down New Street to the Market; then turning left into Lanadwell Street, up to Church Lane, up Ruthys Lane left into Church Street and right to Rosehill; then down High Street to Cross Street, following on into Duke Street, left into Mill Square at the bottom of the hill; then, finally, around onto North Quay and back around onto West Quay, South Quay and the Dock — and, on the way, wandering up a few side streets.

Due to the format of the book, two portrait images leave a lot of blank paper. Where they occur together I have gone back through the proof and inserted other pictures where possible, I hope these do not spoil the reader's perambulation of the town.

Over the years many changes have been recorded in Padstow's local magazine, the *Padstow Echo*. This has been of great service in helping to record the town's modern history. Thanks should go to the editor, Sue Norfolk, and her helpers for continuing the great work that the late Stephen Fuller instigated and Margaret Brenton continued.

Any visitors to the town who are interested in this little book will benefit from a visit to our excellent town museum, which is located in the Padstow Institute. Any local would benefit from attending the Old Cornwall Society meetings held at the Social Club on occasional Wednesday evenings. The meetings are advertised on the OCS board in the Strand, and they have excellent guest speakers. I am a recent convert to the society and am sorry I did not join earlier.

I hope that this book reminds the older generation of how things were, and shows the younger generation how the town has changed.

Malcolm McCarthy
5 Raleigh Close
Padstow

Padstow from Dennis Hill

The top picture shows Dennis Creek as it was before the railway embankment and tracks cut the access off. This creek was at one time a thriving shipyard. The sprawl of the new town is evident, as it has gradually encroached south from the old town along the riparian fields.

Netherton Road

Netherton Road is pictured here before the council houses were built at the southern end. Not long after this picture was taken, the council houses were built in Netherton, Trelawney and Caswarth Terrace, with many local families moving from the damp, cramped conditions of the old town cottages to new purpose-built council houses. Later, the estate spread further up the hill to include Lodenek Avenue and Sarah's Lane, which were completed in the 1960s.

Padstow.

Below Dennis Road, Looking North
The top picture, *c.* 1905, shows a view from the fields where Egerton and Treverbyn Roads meet. Looking across the fields you can see the top of the railway station beside the steam from a train, and beyond is the harbour before the New Pier was built in 1932.

Malt House Corner from the East

On the corner of Dennis Road and New Street was an old building that was previously both a garage and a Malt House. Clemow, the owners of the building, were maltsters, and hop and seed merchants. There was an old pair of cottages attached in New Street, and I remember the building having an interesting round wall. This is the first pair of a series of photos recording this site and the one opposite where Reynolds' Garage stood (both sites were developed at the same time).

Malt House Corner from the North

The garages, which I always knew as a boy as 'Clemow's', and Malt House Corner, looking across the road from the site of the demolished Reynolds' Garage. The garage before demolition is pictured below, and the new houses built on the site can be seen on page 17.

The Old Ambulance Station and Cottages

Looking down the hill from the Lawn Car Park towards Malt House Corner, the old ambulance station and cottages can be seen prior to demolition. The cottages used to be lived in by the Underhill family and the Giddys.

The Board School

The Board School, built in 1876, which is also the year this photo was taken, is shown here before the front playground wall was moved back to accommodate the road. The other photo shows the old school building after its conversion to houses. A new school was built at the top of Grenville Road when today's population became too large for the old one.

Saunders Hill

A mansion built by the Rawling family, merchants, Saunders Hill was later bought and dismantled by the Prideaux family. The house stood on the site of the Padstow Social Club, which was built by local labour and opened 17 December 1988. The steward and deputy steward, pictured outside the front door, always guarantee you a friendly welcome and a good pint.

A View from St Petroc's Gardens

St Petroc's Gardens were walled gardens connected to St Petroc's House, a Rawling family residence, as was St Edmund's House (see page 86). Houses have now been built on these gardens and most of the old walls have been demolished. The view from the gardens across the town is still very similar today, but differences are evident on close inspection.

Hill St, Padstow.

Old Cottages in Hill Street

As a boy I remember going to visit Horace and Mrs Murt and Ben and Mrs Hill. Since then the cottages have been renovated and modernised but still retain their old world charm.

Honey Cottage

Still in Hill Street is the cottage that Mr Honey used to live in. Today the cottage is called Honey Cottage. This cottage has changed very little over the years, and I well remember old Mr Honey living there with a big religious print on the living room wall. The buildings in Hill Street may look the same, but sadly all the local characters that lived in them have died, never to be replaced, and they are much missed.

Cottage on the Corner of New Street and Hill Street

The cottage can be seen in the old photograph as it was *c.* 1900. The front door of the cottage has now been moved into Hill Street.

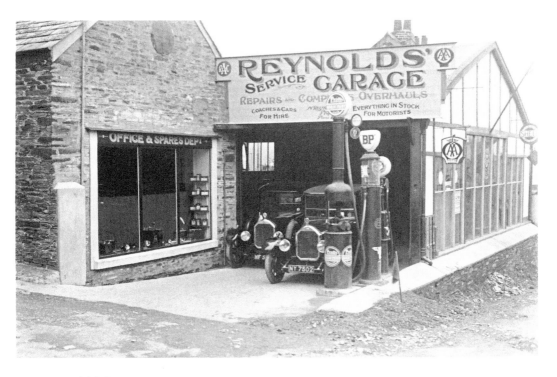

Reynolds' Garage

Reynolds' Garage, developed on the site of an old farmyard, had its office in the old barn that ran along the east side of Hill Street. The garage has since been knocked down and cottages have been built on the site. Reynolds also had a garage in St Edmunds Lane where they kept their Rolls Royce hearse, which was hired out to Mr Blake, undertaker, for funerals.

Looking Down New Street

Looking down New Street, the changes are mainly due to the bomb that fell on Tudor Close during the Second World War. The bomb demolished the old cottages on the right-hand side of the road.

Houses Old and New

Above is a close-up of the ancient cottages in New Street that were, sadly, blown up. They were replaced by the characterless houses pictured below.

Hornabrook Court

This is the first in a series of images showing the Hornabrook blacksmiths shop, which developed into Hornabrook Garage. When the garage was demolished it was replaced with Hornabrook Court. (I felt this area should be thoroughly covered, as it has been such a major change to the centre of town.)

**The Garage Office
taken from the Drang**
Before it was a blacksmith's, this end property — I am reliably informed — was the first Hawkin's butcher's shop, before it moved to the bottom corner of Broad Street.

The Stock Houses, Mill Street

The empty garage site taken from the same spot as the images on the previous page, together with the Stock Houses in Mill Street during demolition in 1987. One pair of Stock Houses still remain, they are tiny one-up one-down properties.

The Old Garage

The shell of the old garage pictured just as I remember it. My grandfather, Bob Johns, worked here for many years and I spent many happy hours exploring the ramshackle upstairs rooms and watching the swifts and swallows darting around the roomy interior, which had an open cliff face at the back of the garage.

Sunfood Stores

Walter Chapman and his sister are pictured outside their Sunfood Stores. This building has changed little, now being The Famous Little Store.

Market Place, Looking North

The top photo was taken in the 1890s, and the buildings are very similar to those we see today, as can be seen below. The style of life was very different then, with stalls in the street and people wandering around the road without fear of being run over — happy times back in the good old days!

Market Place Looking Towards Lanadwell Street

Pictured *c.* 1875, it is interesting to see the shop window boarded up, which must have been a tedious daily task.

The London Inn *c.* 1900
Now the landlords, Mike and Pauline
Meredith, have a wonderful display of
flowers hanging from every available point
on the building, as can be seen below.

The Alms Houses in Middle Street

Now called Tredwen Court, these properties are owned and managed by the Padstow Poor Lands Charities and are lived in by single persons over the age of fifty. The properties were extended and reopened by Peter Prideaux Brune on 18 January 1989.

The Back of Thomas Henwoods Mill, Mill Road
The building has since been converted into flats with car parking below, but it still retains its rough industrial character.

Padstow Gas Company Gas Works

This is a photograph of the Padstow Gas Company gas works, which were on the site of Ladywell old people's flats. After the gasworks were demolished the site was, for many years, a public car park next to the Public Rooms, at that time Padstow Fire Station. I can well remember the big green gasometer behind the car park in my youth.

Tony Fuller

Tony Fuller ran a shoe repair business in Mrs Hackey Brown's lean to, and many a time as a boy I ran down to see him to have a pair of shoes mended or a school satchel re-stitched. He was always cheerful, despite his disability, and would talk about Padstow United football club with great relish. He was also a good water polo player and I well remember him playing in matches in the Inner Quay. The bottom photo is St John's Methodist chapel, which was sadly demolished in 1987. Grace Magor opened the new chapel in September 1988.

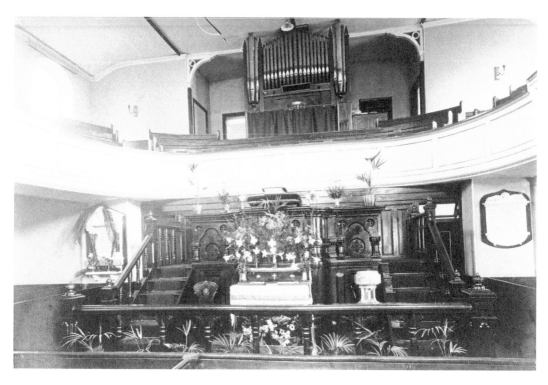

St John's Chapel

The inside of St John's chapel taken on its centenary in 1927 and, below, during its demolition sixty years later. What a terrible shame that this structurally sound, beautiful building should be sacrificed to make room for a car park.

St John's Chapel

The site of St John's chapel and the car park that now replaces it. The new chapel is now in the old St John's hall, which juxtaposed the original chapel building and was used for Sunday schools and tea treats.

Church Lane

Church Lane in the days when only local people lived down town, as it happens this is one of the few corners of the old town where a few locals still live.

Church Street

The top two photos compare Church Street looking down towards Duke Street, while the bottom picture shows the top of Church Street, which has changed very little in the 100 years since this photo was taken.

Rosehill, High Street
Once the home of Dr Harvey and his family, Rosehill has recently been sympathetically refurbished and is an example to all on how to keep the character of a property whilst making it suitable for modern living.

High Street

Looking down High Street, there are now two small estates where the gardens of the Nook and the Bird Gardens used to be, hence the drastic changes on the left-hand side of modern picture.

The Local Undertaker's

Mr W. A. Blake, undertaker, outside his workshop *c.* 1911, the year he bought the business from Mr Magor. The same building today, and below the new Chapel of Repose, built and run by Mr Blake's great nephew and great great nephews, Terry and Martin Rogers, who have carried on the family undertaking business. The building was dedicated on 28 Nov 1992 by Revd Ron Hockley, the previous chapel of rest being beside St John's chapel, which was tragically demolished along with the chapel in 1987.

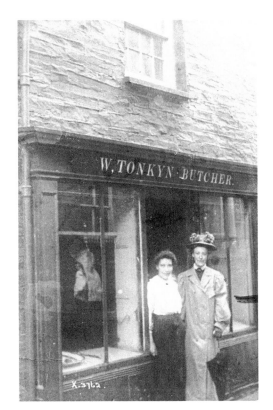

Tonkyns' Butcher's Shop, Church Street
Mrs Tonkyn at the butcher's shop in Church Street. The shop, after having a new front, was for several years a launderette.

Looking Down Duke Street from Cross Street

The two shops are now residential and the houses are a little spruced up, but otherwise there is little physical change to the scene.

Duke Street

The top picture shows the properties on the bank in Duke Street as they were in 1920, and the following four pictures catalogue the changes to two neighbouring properties. These changes are ongoing, as, even as I write, the front of the property below is boarded up for renovation.

Duke Street

Nancarrows shop, top left, has been skilfully converted back to a house by Paul Brunyee during 2009. The bottom two pictures are of Owen Bakers, which is now Padstow Studio, owned and run by artist Sarah Adams.

Looking from Duke Street down Middle Street

Miss Stribley's shop on the right is now Stein's Café. I well remember this shop as Mrs Joyce Clark's haberdashery in my youth. Molly Pinch, the shop assistant, as I recall, was constantly bustling around the shop. Always busy and cheerful, she was a real Padstow character.

Duke Street
These two images, taken from the market and looking up Duke Street, clearly illustrate the drastic changes to both sides of this end of Duke Street.

The Arcade

The bottom two images show the cottages where the Arcade is and the Arcade as it is now.

The Post Office
The oldest known photograph taken in Padstow, the post office photographed in 1852 stands on the site of the present day Barclays Bank. The terracotta horsemen mentioned on page 96 stood on top of these buildings.

Tonkyns' Butcher's Shop

The shop is pictured after it moved from the Church Street premises. Outside the shop proudly stand Bill Ploughman, Fred Dale, Mr Tonkyn the butcher, and his son Arthur. The building now houses a sandwich shop.

Blake's Shop in Mill Square

In my youth it was Miss Old's quaint little shop, but today it has become incorporated into the Clipper Restaurant. The land, which was once road, is now fenced off and, claimed by the Clipper, used for tables and chairs, a practice that is also happening outside of Walker's fish and chip restaurant. We are slowly losing little public bits of our town — beware!

Rojano's Pizza House
The present-day Rojano's Pizza House as it was back in 1905, at which time it was a private house.

Tonkin's boot and shoe shop
Marjorie Hutchins standing outside Tonkin's boot and shoe shop in Mill Square in 1923, the left-hand corner is now part of Rojano's Pizza House and the rest is part of a surf clothing shop.

Mill Square Looking onto North Quay
The old photograph shows the old shop front, left, and cottage, right. The cottage was an ancient building with carved and painted ships' beams built into it. The Cory Memorial Shelter is now on the site of the cottage.

Harbour Ices

This beautifully slated cottage has been replaced by a shop with a flat above. The shop opened this summer as an ice cream parlour with a fantastic array of flavours.

The Jackie Stanley Estate Agency

The present day Jackie Stanley Estate Agency building is shown in the 1890s, when Mr Faull, the blind Wesleyan organist, lived here. He is shown here talking to the Wesleyan minister, and the window is full of plants. Below, Ham and Jendens Harbour Café; this quaint old building, despite at one time being condemned, has survived the ravages of time with little change.

The Old Cottage at the Entrance to Mill Square

Looking back along North Quay, the photograph above shows the old cottage at the entrance to Mill Square *c.* 1895. I couldn't take a modern photograph during the summer due to the number of people that now visit the town, one of the biggest changes we have seen over the last thirty years. The bottom photograph was taken at the end of September after the town had quietened down considerably.

The Strand

Looking over Langfords Steps towards the Strand, many obvious changes are evident in this pair of photos.

Langfords Steps Viewed from the South

The long low building that was then a tea room is now a restaurant. During its life it has been the North Cornwall Bank, Langfords Insurance Agency and Consulate, the Electricity Showrooms and a fish and chip shop.

The Shipwrights Inn

The Shipwrights Inn is pictured here as it was in the 1860s, when outside it was a sawpit. Baulks of timber were seasoned in the Inner Basin or log pools, before being cut into planks by the sawyers in the sawpits. An enormous number of planks would have been required during the port's busy shipbuilding days. The lower picture shows the building as it was in the 1920s, when H. Brown, painter and decorator, was using it. Now the pit is gone and the building is the Shipwrights Inn public house.

The Fishermen's Mission

The top photo, taken when the Red Brick Building was being demolished, shows the wooden Fishermen's Mission building in front, which was demolished at the same time. The Fishermen's Mission was a place where local and visiting fishermen could relax between trips or during bad weather; the bottom picture shows the inside of the building.

The Red Brick Building

The red brick building, pictured, fell into a derelict state; a public enquiry deemed it dangerous and it was knocked down. The new red brick building that replaces it was built in a similar style and is split into flats. The building was not always this shape, as many wrongly believe, as can be seen in the photograph on page 63.

Brabyn's Yard

Brabyn's Yard boatbuilding sheds and offices are pictured in a state of decay. This little quay has been a boatyard since it was built, and when Carter was running the yard in the 1830s the entrance had gates to keep it wet and full of water when required. Now it has been fenced off and expensive flats built on the site of the old boatyard buildings.

Boatyards

The top photo shows Brabyn's Yard when it was in use for ship repairs. Ship building and repair has been a tradition in Padstow for centuries, and of late it has been kept alive at the huge blue building on the town council's railway land. The bottom photo is of Tony Conium's netter *Diadem* when she was on the then A&J Marine slip. This yard has just changed hands again and we can only hope that ship building and repair continues to be an all-year-round employer in Padstow.

A view of the Quay from Mount Pleasant in the Early 1860s
The old Red Brick Building, before it assumed its familiar shape, is evident in the photograph below. The quays and waterfront on the far side of the quay, as illustrated in the bottom picture, look completely different today.

The Long Lugger

A seat where old men used to sit and while their time away, today the Long Lugger has been replaced by a row of benches. During the summer months these benches are normally packed with fish-and-chip-eating day-trippers.

Quay Gaps

Looking from the entrance to Mill Square east to the Quay Gaps before the entrance was restricted by the building of extended southern arm of the Inner Basin, which encompasses a sewage holding sump. The bottom photo, taken in April 1989 when the capping was being finished, shows the gate and shuttering. The gate is now used to retain water and keeping the quay wet and the boats afloat. However, this is not what it was built for, as it was built along with raising the walls on Langfords Quay to prevent the town flooding on the equinoxial spring tides.

Looking Across from North Quay to the Strand
The image taken in the 1860s and that of the present day are very different, the whole of the western side of the quay being completely rebuilt since this early photo was taken.

West Quay

A slightly later view of the West Quay, but this image, taken around 1900, is not recognisable as the quay we know pictured below.

West Quay Continued
1920, the quay is becoming slightly more recognisable, compare with the photo below.

Looking Along West Quay Towards North Quay

This view today is slightly different, as pontoons have been put in along this wall; the bottom photo was taken during the eclipse, when, as berthing master, I managed to cram ninety-six visiting vessels into the Inner Harbour.

'Thunderbolt Alley'

Market Strand on a high tide and as it is now. The left-hand side of this lane is the old market house. Originally the Shambles, it was built around a courtyard that used to have double doors opening into the present day Market Place. The bottom photo was taken in the 1860s before Bray and Parkyns mill building, now the Custom House Hotel, was built on the corner of South Quay and Riverside.

The Lobster Pot

Mrs Grace Soper outside of her wet fish shop; this shop is now the Lobster Pot and is always changing what it sells, this year it has been a clothes shop.

Padstow Angling Centre and Bin Two

The top photo shows Mrs Brunyee's derelict cottage backing on to the Drang, which was rebuilt as Strand House. The top half of Strand House is now a bed and breakfast, and the bottom two shops contain the Padstow Angling Centre and Bin Two, our local wine shop — two excellent shops and both well worth a visit.

Looking Across at the Strand from the Tidal Gate
The whole feel of the harbour has changed and this is clearly illustrated by these photographs. The top photograph is from the days of sail, dating from 1905.

FISHING FLEET
PADSTOW

Steam Trawlers Inside the Inner Basin in the 1920s

The lower photo shows the modern-day beam trawlers taken about ten years ago. They used to visit the port between January and the end of April for the Trevose Season, fishing for Dover sole. Of late, we have had dramatically less trawlers due to decommissioning of the fleet and the closing of the fishing grounds off Padstow.

South Quay
An early view of South Quay and the same view today.

Harbour Inn

The top photos are of the Harbour Inn at the lower end of Strand Street, as can be seen this building has changed little. The bottom photo is taken outside of the Harbour Inn when the circus came during the 1930s; the elephants were brought down to the quay to bathe.

Three Images of the South Quay

Pictured are three photographs of the south quay: top left, 1860s; bottom, 1950s; and one of the present day.

South Quay

A series of four photos, the earliest from the 1860s showing the arm of the Inner Quay, which was then called the Pier; beyond it to the south was the beach and foreshore. By the time the second photograph was taken, the cottages on the corner have been replaced with the large, square mill building. The shipyard is visible in the distance, with its two basins. The ship's mast sticking up behind the roofs of the houses illustrates the vast size of these quays.

South Quay

The top photograph was taken *c.* 1905; by this time the railway had arrived and filled in the southern most dock using the shipyard wall as a retaining wall. The railway station has now been built on the old shipyard, and all the buildings along Riverside have been demolished to make way for the railway tracks. Court House has been shortened and the harbour changed forever. The bottom photo, though not showing much, does illustrate all the land that has been reclaimed where the South Quay car park now stands with the new Harbour Office and dock beyond.

The Corner of the South Quay and Riverside

Close-up photographs of the corner of the South Quay and Riverside illustrate some of the changes over time. The top photograph shows the Custom House *c.* 1860, its own quay and gig on davits. The gig is hanging over the present-day road and the cottages both to its left and right can clearly be seen, these have long since been demolished. The bottom picture is taken after Court House has been shortened for the railway tracks to come along Riverside but before the foreshore has been reclaimed.

The Corner of the South Quay

By 1952, when the top photograph was taken, the road and car park had been built, and this photograph gives us a good idea of how the sand dredgers operated. The lower picture shows how tourism has pushed industrialism out, the sand operations now moving to the outer dock allowing this arm of the quay to be used as a car park, which is patronised mainly by visitors to the town.

Padstow Harbour Office

This slipway ran alongside the arm of the Inner Basin, with nothing but water beyond it. These days we have the car park with the Harbour Office and beyond that a 700-foot long dock, which was built in 1911 to accommodate the visiting fishing fleet.

The Memorial Hall on Riverside
The Memorial Hall building is now Padstow's official village hall and well used by local groups.

Avery's Row

Mr and Mrs Fuller in their cottage at the top of Avery's Row before the cottages were rebuilt. The same scene is pictured below but taken in August 1993, which was before the old sail loft building was refurbished.

Inside the Sail Loft

This photograph shows the inside of the loft at the top of the steps in August 1993 when it was being used as a fishermen's store by David Evans. The room would have been a sail loft and for a while it was Leonard Williams' funeral director's workshop. This building has been refurbished now, the steps have gone and the property has been turned into accommodation.

St Edmunds House in St Edmunds Lane, Then Horsemill Lane

Anna Rawling is walking in the garden, her younger sister Caroline sitting on the window seat inside the house. This dates this photograph to pre-November 1857, when Anna died, and at this time their brother, Henry Peter, a magistrate, held court in the house. The bottom picture shows the same property today; it has been split into little cottages, which are rented out by Rick Stein. Fortunately, the renovation of this property has been sympathetically carried out.

Rick Stein's Restaurant

Brad Trethewey's removals and storage unit has now been transformed into Rick Stein's famous The Seafood Restaurant, which had a new foyer extension and a refurbishment after the 2007 season.

The Railway Land

A photo taken from the area outside the present-day Padstow Cycle Hire shed, looking towards the harbour and showing the railway land and buildings. This is compared with a view of the same place, but taken from Style Field, which shows the dramatic changes to the area, if from the opposite direction.

The Fishermen's Stores

Looking along the dock to the north, the two old runs of fish buyer's offices and fishermen's stores and the weighbridge in the distance can clearly be seen. These stores have been rebuilt by Padstow Harbour Commissioners and the new sheds are used by the local fishermen; funding was available in the form of grant aid to facilitate this project. The local fishermen manage these stores through the Padstow Fishermen's Co-operative.

The Fish Market

The fish market was sandwiched between railway tracks, where fish were packed in goods wagons for transporting to London for Billingsgate market, and the Dock, where the trawlers landed their catch. The Southern Railway ran the fish market. The modern photo is taken from the same spot, but the scene has somehow lost its charm.

The Old Kipper House Building

A remnant of the days of the herring drifters, the old Kipper House building was where Scottish fisherwomen would come and work during the herring season. This building is where the split herrings were smoked and made into kippers. The new building, which retains the basic shape of the old concrete building, is the National Lobster Hatchery and used to cultivate juvenile lobsters for release back into the sea.

Padstow Harbour from the North

This pair of images show the difference between Riverside and quays of the 1870s and the present day, viewed from Brabyn's Yard, looking south. I am sure that you will see numerous dramatic changes if you play spot the difference.

The Padstow to Rock Ferry

Pictured *c.* 1910, William Henry Baker, the ferryman, is sporting his long sea boots. The lower photo shows the *Black Tor Two* on the purpose built Ferry Slip and the older *Black Tor* ferry coming alongside her. *Black Tor Two* is the first Black Rock ferry to have a covered area to protect the passengers against inclement weather.

Reynolds Bus to Trevone

Compare this bus to the buses of today. The bus terminus is beside the Padstow Town Council Offices, which were the old Station House. The busses at the terminus are the normal green greyhound ones plus a red London Bus, which runs from Newquay occasionally.

The Old Oss

The Old Oss and its followers pose on the steps of Abbey House c. 1905. 2009, and the Old Oss at Prideaux Place is pictured again although its look has changed, the skirt shortened and the face on its hat changed. The band has grown enormously from those days of a century ago, although the custom is basically continued in the same manner and with the same passion, although now followed by huge throngs of people.

The Terracotta Horsemen
The terracotta horsemen who from time immemorial have stood on the property at the north side the Market. They supposedly advertise a place where you could get a change of horse — or so rumour has it. Very sadly, the new owners of Barclays Bank took them down. However, they were rescued from the skip, apparently by one of the bank's employees, and can be viewed in Padstow Museum, which is well worth a visit in its own right.

Acknowledgements

Lambert Dive, Michael Champion, George Barnes, Sheila McCarthy, Lionel McCarthy, Pat McCarthy, Rodney Bate, Pat Bate, Tony Allen, Guy Pompa, Mrs Leonard Prior, John Buckingham, Martin and Terry Rogers, Rob Atkinson and Betty King.